# Prisons to Paradise - My Journey to Christ

Janel Tufts

BookLeaf Publishing

Presentation by *BookLeaf Publishing*

Web: www.bookleafpub.com

E-mail: info@bookleafpub.com

ISBN: 9789357747295

First edition 2023

*I dedicate this book to anyone, feeling lost, hopeless, or scared. To those who find themselves in situations they never thought they would be in; doing things they never thought they would do; or, being involved with people they never thought they would know. You have the power inside you to overcome whatever you are facing. If you look within and be honest with yourself, you will heal. Life WILL get better. You will always have to work for it but there IS hope.*

# ACKNOWLEDGEMENT

I would like to thank God, Spirit, Universe, Source for always protecting me, guiding me and showing me the power within.

I would also like to thank my family for never giving up on me. My three amazing boys, for always giving me a reason to persevere and strive to do better. I would also like to thank all the people I have crossed paths with for coming into my life for teaching me, inspiring me or encouraging me on my healing path.

# PREFACE

The poems within this book are a compilation of the soul-searching to truly identify who it is I am, outside of the opinions I've carried from other people, outside of limiting beliefs that I put on myself as a means of protection, and the beautiful journey of coming back to who it is I really am and what I believe.

# Prison

Prison, an interesting word I truly believe.
The meaning can vary, it's what you conceive.
Some see an institution, a place for bad guys.
But what of the child, afraid and told lies?
Offered a life by parents in strife; always hoping
for a joyful life.
Making wishes upon the stars.
Wounded and broken by childhood scars.
Fighting and anger, fear and demise.
This child lies still and builds a disguise.
Who they see themselves inside,
Of dreams and love, and happy times.
Though the years go by,
Ever wishing they'd just fly.
Each day is scary and just drags by.
Abuse and neglect start a ripple effect.
For sadness and longing of their basic needs,
Caused years of frustration,
Self-doubt, tears, and self-destruction.
This child who only tried to love and survive,
Spent their life living in compromise.
Always avoiding conflict and confrontation.
Trying to conform, it's self-mutilation.
Decades go by and still they try,
Believing it'll get better before they die.

Always a smile, a laugh, or a hand,
To cheer someone up, assist with a plan.
Kindness and love inside of this being,
Trapped forever until they start seeing,
Who they are or what the future could be.
This is the true meaning of prison, if you ask
me.

# Playground

Be true to you, don't lie to yourself.
See all there is to see, from the darkest corner to
the highest shelf.
There's nothing there you shouldn't find.
This makes up all you are, so just be kind.
As you look inside, don't be scared.
Embrace it all you're meant to share,
The pain, the hurt, the healing you found.
Your love, your strength, your faith- that sweet,
sweet sound,
Of the little you full of hope, dreams, and
ambition.
A pure little soul tuned into their life's mission.
Not a care in the world. Remember that child?
Imagination, free-spirit, you were born to be
wild.
Before you learned fear, hate, and rejection.
Your soul's purpose was fun and reflection.
To live in the moment, present with peace.
Exploring, observing, create and release.
Living each day with curiosity and wonder.
Not living in fear, afraid to blunder.
Enjoy life the way it was meant to be,
Embracing yourself, until you see.
All the places to explore and people to meet;

Joy to have and opportunities to greet.
Choose love, live light, be present now.
Feel, accept, and release, even when you don't
see how.
Intuition guides your body and faith your mind.
Trust in yourself and always be kind.
For in my journey, this is what I found,
Your inner child will guide you to life's
playground.

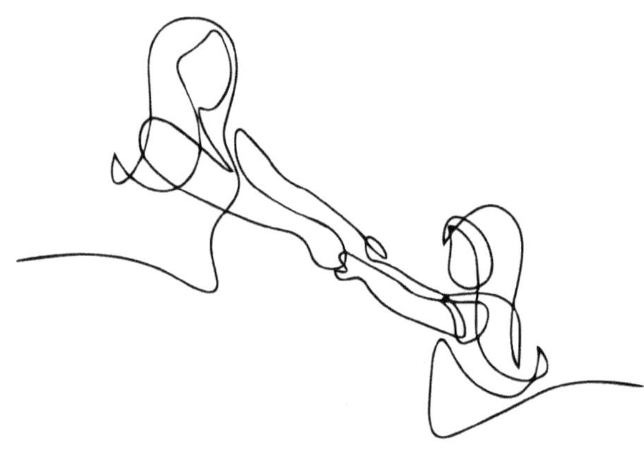

# A Child's Truth

A child was born with a light in their soul.
Into a world of challenges, destructive and cold.
A life that left the young feeling old.
"It's life, deal with it," is what they are told.
"Get out of the way, grow up, don't play."
"Shut up, you're stupid," you hear them say.
"Stop it, you fool, get out of the way."
These words stayed with you, even today.
Like seeds that have been planted,
Time goes by, we take it for granted,
That what we plant is destined to grow.
Like it or not, we see, or it sows.
The tragedy is, it's not just from then.
Then turns to now, fuel added by men.
Pain, hurt, neglect, abuse…
Sometimes feeling it's no use.
We all walk a path unique to us,
Teaching us lessons, making us cuss.
What you choose to do in moments so blue,
Will open the door and give you the clue.
Everything in life is up to you.
Hope, love, and a future that's new.
See it, believe it, know it's true.
Pick yourself up, see life anew.
Look within, find your reason to push through.

We all have a gift, we're waiting to share.
Not everyone is cruel, some truly care.

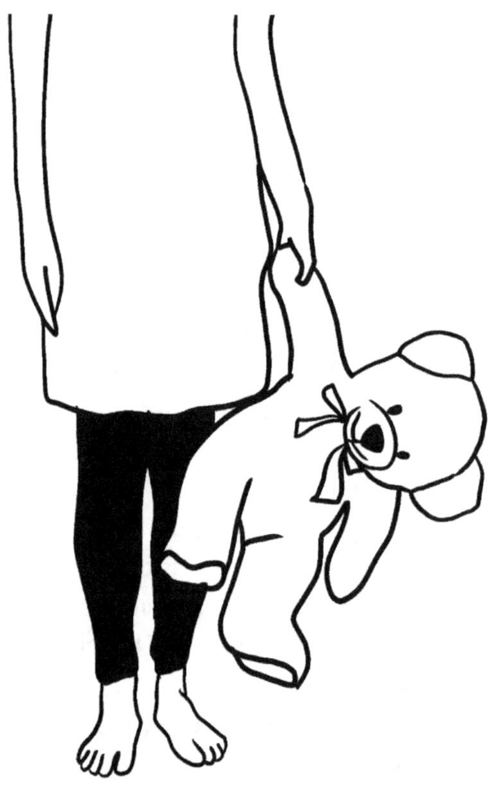

# Breaking Chains

In a world full of hurt, pain, and regret.
We can barely focus, everything's a threat.
From bills, food, and transportation…
To relationships, health, and reputation.
The horrible things people have said,
Stick like glue to thoughts in our head.
Try as we might, to barely scrape by,
Collections are calling, accounts are dry.
The weight of the world only gets heavier,
And inside, we only feel emptier.
Add the death of those we care about,
Increase the agony, grief, and doubt.
Employment issues come into play.
You just pray they're not here to stay.
Relationships end, court cases begin.
Struggles are here, again and again.
But through it all, a hope remains,
That someday soon we'll break these chains.

# Searching

Have you ever felt like this before?
Where you just can't get yourself off the floor.
When your world is crashing all around.
And your hope is nowhere to be found.
Take a pause and breathe.
See what it is you need to free.
For only then, can you truly see,
Who it is, you are meant to be.
When you feel as though all hope is gone,
Remember who it is this world belongs.
You are the master creator, a human God.
Do not pretend, as if this is the end.
Thoughts are powerful, unbridled and free.
Unique to us all, the perspective we see.
The limits encountered and the panic we face,
Are set in our minds in those final goodbyes.
Be kind to yourself, body and soul.
But treasure your mind, and thoughts tenfold,
For here is the key to your reality.
Imagine, create, dream, and believe.
The more you see, the more to believe.
The universe is you, and also is me.
We are now living the sum
Of every single thought and feeling we hold,
Think happy, stay positive, and spread your joy,

To everyone and anyone you chance to meet.
For in that connection, you plant the seed,
Of hope and love, a future we need.

# Healing

From the darkest past, come the purest souls.
The ones who love and see high goals.
Who care and forgive and never give up.
Regardless of trials or pain filling their cup.
Who look for the positive, anything good.
Removing, replacing where pain once stood.
To look within and see the fears,
And realize they're from the past, the former years.
You are today what you want to be.
The lesson here you have to see,
Inside you find the answers you seek.
Pause, listen, take a peek.
You're not the things they said to you.
That is simply their point of view.
Although physically, you barely survived,
God had plans for you, fiercely contrived.
Focus on how far you've come, be proud, this is you.
Listen to the voice, this is your queue.
Love yourself in every way,
But please don't forget to pray,
For every circumstance you made it through,
And each person's lesson, meant to keep you true.

For this path you're heading on lies your destiny.
Will you be honest enough to really see?

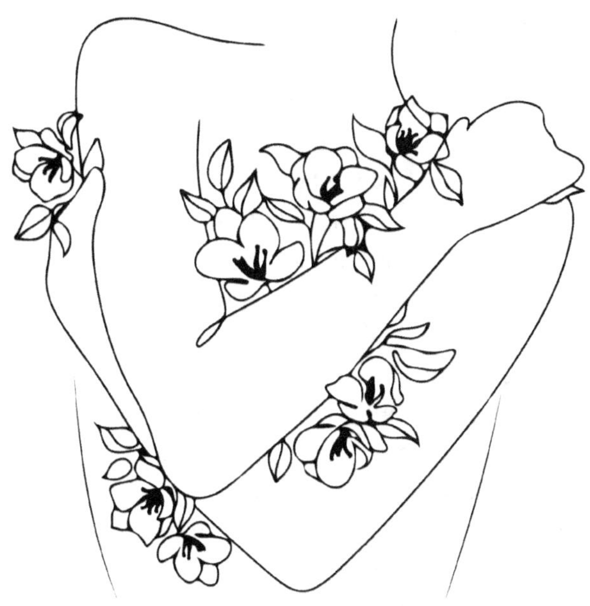

# Faith

Faith is listening to your voice inside,
And knowing it is not your pride.
But your guiding light in the universe.
The path you're on has been rehearsed.
Before you were born, here on Earth,
You were well aware of your worth.
The goals you had, and lessons to learn.
Battles to fight, you had to yearn.
So have faith and remember now,
Who you are, find the how.
Do not question when or why.
Simply know, and you will fly.
Out of the ashes, and into the light,
Like a phoenix rising in the dead of night.
To rise above all the gloom,
And allow this bud to finally bloom.
To show the world who you really are.
You speak your truth, near and far.
Beyond the scars, regret, and shame,
Built a solid foundation and sturdy frame.
Now imagine, dream, and construct,
For you've endured, loved, and never gave up.
Karma, Dharma, Yin and Yang.
What goes out comes back again.

# What is Love?

Love is kind, it does not hurt.
There is no judgment, it kindly asserts,
A voice of encouragement, or a helping hand.
Love does not cause fear, or drown you with
sand.
It holds you and comforts you,
When you are weak and feeling blue.
Never does love manipulate,
Belittle you or make you the bait.
Love will only heal you, help you find peace.
Never make you question, or call the police.
It is gentle, tender, and forgiving.
Not pain, nor fear in living.
Love is abundant and will catalyze,
Everything once you realize,
Control and abuse, even when in disguise,
Is sweetness all wrapped up in lies.
Do not be fooled I plead so true,
This love is inside of you.
A little spark, it may be; it never fades,
And as you see, it grows in waves.
The more love you have for you,
The Universe sees, the world does too.
Boundaries established to protect your love,
Ready to move forward to fly like a dove.

Knowing what love is not,
This is the key to loving what you've got.

15

# Truth

The day I looked within myself to find my
purpose,
I finally truly saw all the ways they tried to
usurp us.
God cleared the fog and opened my eyes,
And after all of this time, I finally realize,
What life is, and how God works.
This dawning comes with so many perks!
From darkness to light and dim to bright,
I am grateful now to just be me.
A child of God with faith to just be.
Creating a life full of possibility.
Finding who I am and taking responsibility,
To understand and take control of my life,
Fills me with hope to continue free of strife.
The release of fear, regret, and shame.
Glory to God, praise his name!
From this day forward His servant I am.
I'll proudly say I am part of His clan.
Forgiveness is found after coming to terms,
With digging through the past to uncover the
worms.
For within you, is the garden God prepped.
Long before you took your first step.
He protected you and guided you,

He carried you through.
You didn't know how loved you really are,
And the fact is, you're God's shining star!

# I am Marriage

I am marriage.
I am many things to many people.
My definition has changed as decades past,
And it seems today I rarely last.
Many people say, "goodbye..."
Before their vows, until we die.
To see a love like yours survive,
Gives hope to all and keeps me alive.
I have seen it all through the years,
Blooming love, new life appears.
Joy, tenderness and elation.
The hope, the dreams, the anticipation.
As newness ebbs and life sets in,
Struggles are there again and again.
The ups and downs in constant motion,
So much so it's like the ocean.
Injuries heal and illnesses pass.
Memories are made in your Looking Glass.
Good times come, and bad times too.
How you focus is up to you.
Children, work, financial burdens...
At times there's just no herdin',
The overwhelming, highs and lows
That seem to keep you on your toes.

I've seen with you, compassion and caring.
Simple things, is that so daring?
Forgiveness and kindness, loving compromise.
These are qualities of no small size.
To give of yourself in so many ways,
Just to see a smile singing of praise.
Effort and time, it takes devotion.
You two exemplify this with such emotion.
I smile upon you, 60 years of commitment.
Not to mention, 60+ years of love to go with it.
Inspiration to all, is what you've been,
Impacting the lives of your family and friends.

# Around the Corner

How are you always happy?
A question I'm asked so often.
I reflect on the need for the heart to soften.
Letting go of all the pain and sorrow.
Negativity, whether from you or them.
Don't forget, there's always tomorrow.
You're not what you've survived or where
you've been.
This person you are, is faithful and strong.
Don't focus on opinions, mistakes, and sorrows.
You're here to experience, there's no right or
wrong.
Follow your heart, your inner child, there's no
need to borrow.
That which doesn't belong to you.
Separate yourself and search your soul.
Holding on to negativity surely takes a toll,
Don't forget, acknowledge your
accomplishments, give credit for what you do.
On who it is you're meant to be,
And what it is the world should see.
You are constantly evolving.
Ever seeking and solving,
Where you went wrong and how to get better.
You release that which doesn't belong in a letter,

Send it to God with hopes and prayers,
Knowing He's the ONLY one who truly cares.
You released your fear, judgment, and worry,
Allowing your blessings to come in in a flurry.
You are no longer in a frantic race,
Everyone can see it in your face.
No longer a foreigner.
Full of hope, knowing change is just around the
corner.

# Me

Silly, goofy, happy me.
This is who I choose to be.
I am loved and uniquely me,
No matter what others choose to see.
It does not matter what life holds.
I choose love, and to break the molds,
Of things people told me and what I could do.
Society, religion, my family, too.
Limits, boxes, people's definitions,
Do not accept these tragic conditions.
Life is yours, it doesn't belong to them.
You've got to decide the where and when.
Of truly what is possible and what is not.
Look around and see, what it is you've been
taught.
Search to identify the things you sought.
Be honest with yourself if you truly want to win.
This takes courage to look back at where you've
been.
Knowing full well, you didn't think you'd make
it out,
Of the pain, the hurt, the perpetual blackout.
But now looking back, don't be sad or have
regrets.
You've overcome, you beat the bets;

Of every person, obstacle, and situation,
Who thought they'd control your outcome, your
destination.
But be proud of who you are and what you've
done.
Take inventory of every lesson, do not run.
Face the emotion, all the fear and pain,
Guilt, shame, embarrassment, and blame.
Don't react, recognize.
These opinions were viewed from other people's
eyes,
Who did not see all the deceit and lies.
Sit, be still, and simply observe.
Soon it'll all be reduced to words.
Here is the point of reckoning.
Can you hear the truth, beckoning?
You are not what they said you are,
But an undeniable shining star.
You overcome each and every ugly situation,
In which you thought it was your life's
destination.
You chose to think bigger, to move toward
better.
You won't stay stuck, you go-getter.
Love yourself, empathize, and just be proud.
You stayed true, standing apart from the crowd.
Always believing, was your way to cope.
But through everything, this gave you hope.
To pick yourself up and shake yourself off.

Instead of choosing simply to scoff.
It won't happen overnight, but this you know,
Like any fruitful garden, it takes time, and you
must sow,
Each and every seed you need, to enjoy the
crops as they grow.
See now is the time you must decide.
Who it is you see inside?
Silly, goofy, happy me.
This is who I choose to be.

# History or Manipulation?

What is really going on in this world today?
As you look around, nothing is truly as they say.
From food to science,
Education, laws, and reasons to be biased.
Follow the rules and do what you're told.
Do not question or dare get bold.
We'll guide you and tell you what to think.
Do not research or question the stink.
It's for your own good, the reasons they state.
You're ignorant, you can't decide your own fate.
You simply would not understand
Or you'd fight if you knew what we planned.
It's centuries old, this war we're in.
History has been manipulated.
God, where do we begin?
From time to space, they've set the pace.
Lying and hiding; the truth will come out.
Religion is their veil, without a doubt.
Facts have been hidden.
The truth is forbidden.
They poison us in every way, in subtle ways
throughout the day.
Spirituality, physiology, and submission.
To deceive and lie to us, is their life's mission.
For our protection… they build a fortress,

To hide their actions from the people.
In the name of the blind, weak, and feeble.
Those who they fear will discover the truth.
Numb them and dumb them, start with the youth.
Subconscious messages, lies straight out of the gate.
If you never know, they can decide our fate.

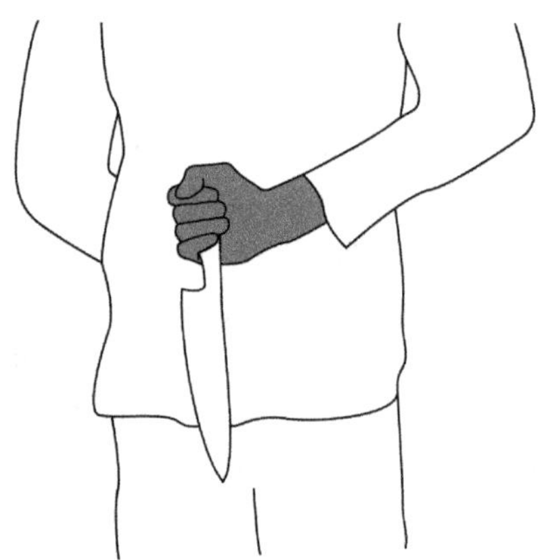

# Grace

Purity, peace, and love.
It's God's grace, I'm writing of.
Appreciating the canvas He painted above, All
of His beauty fits like a glove.
I see His vision in my mind.
A world in which humanity and nature are
combined.
In unity, harmony, so perfectly refined.
To realize we are one. We're all aligned.
Each having a gift meant to assist in His
purpose.
It's not our job to be part of the circus.
He's protecting and guiding, not trying to hurt
us.
God grants us His love and habeas corpus.
You'll find his presence all around.
Call on Him, and it'll be found.
So fear not, and just calm down.
He will not turn and let you drown.
In this situation, you find yourself breaking.
Your emotions are crazy, and your body is
shaking.
You feel as if your heart is aching,
For something more than your efforts are
making.

God will not force or make demands.
He gave us free will over these lands.
When you ask Him finally, to free your hands,
You'll feel peace as your life expands.
The bold and brilliant sunrise,
Almost seems to symbolize,
How you look through God's eyes.
It's about time for you to realize,
Just how deeply loved you are.
Heaven and Earth, both near and far,
It is you who sets the bar.
According to God, you're not a mar.
For you, my dear, are His shining star.

# Change

Change is always around the corner,
So do not fear or be a mourner.
There's so much more life to live.
You have so much to show the world, so much
more to give.
If you find yourself sad, scared, or confused,
Broken, abused, and afraid to get used,
Don't give up hope, faith is the key.
For the future and the change, you hope to see.
All good things in life take a little time.
Please be patient, endure the climb.
There are things we must learn,
If we are to earn.
The peace, love, and joy we desire.
Remove all pain and regret, set it on fire.
Free yourself from the past.
All the guilt and shame that's been amassed.
It does not define who you are.
Don't let it fester and become a scar.
You are beauty and grace,
And you will win the race.
With your head held high,
Comes a peaceful sigh.
No longer in your life are you the foreigner,
For you know, change is just 'round the corner'

# Hope

Hope is always here.
No matter how deafening the silence you hear.
When you feel you are all alone
As if your chances are all blown.
Shake yourself off and pick yourself up.
You have the ability to fill your own cup.
All that you seek, you will find within.
Validation and love, your beautiful grin.
You must find it and give it to yourself first,
Or every relationship will only get worse.
You cannot give what you do not have,
Attempting to apply a salve,
Temporarily covering the wound, hiding the
pain.
Eventually to find out, it was all done in vain.
Get to the root of your frustration.
Accept it all with no hesitation.
You will notice you're a little less tense.
Step-by-step, it starts to make sense.
How all of this confusion, all this worry,
Gave you blinders, your vision became blurry.
Your soul knew it didn't belong.
But the world kept saying this was your song.
You now hear your voice, it's different from
theirs.

It knows your truth, you know it cares.
It shows you the truth in all situations.
Saving you hurt, creating foundations.
Of dreams for the future to heal like a suture.
Allowing the knowledge of a future so clear,
As long as you remember, hope is always near.

# Identity

Who am I?
On what is it that I rely?
For years I thought I was just being shy.
Timid and meek, wishing to fly.
Falling in line, making peace, not wanting to
pry.
Blending in was my grandest lie.
Working hard, barely getting by.
Seeing more to this life in my mind's eye.
More for this world, more to apply.
But every time I try to see the blue sky,
Someone comes in to make me cry.
I've had enough, this is my final goodbye.
I promise my dreams to no longer standby.
From this point on, hear my war cry.
I no longer fear being seen as the bad guy.
I will stand up for myself, and when they ask
why?
Because God told me, "There's more to life than
they imply."
Staying true to myself, with God nearby.
I will clean up myself, a dusty pigsty.
Then God gives me a quick spin dry.
Good as new, no longer tongue-tied.
I come back to the question of who am I.

A beautiful creature meant to fly.
Pure and perfect in God's eye.

# God's Rising Phoenix

Warm summer days, your hearts singing with
praise.
Never could you be broken, from God these
words were spoken.
Have faith, my resilient child.
I know the path has been broken and wild,
But you found the fight to follow through,
On the purpose and path I created for you.
You stayed honest, loyal, and kind.
Even though others would've gone out of their
mind.
You faced every challenge with a smile on your
face.
Taking a deep breath, readjusting your pace.
To be the best person, you could see at the time..
Regardless of the mountains this forced you to
climb.
I've seen all the trails you forged on the way.
Staying true to yourself, no matter what they
say.
The joy you spread and the love you share,
Proves to all, how much you care.
I'm so proud of you, blessed one.
Your light, my dear outshines the sun.
Follow the path that leads to your destiny.

Enjoy, be happy, and live life expectantly.
I'll show you peace, legitimately.
A love that knows no bounds, infinitely.
I love you, my precious child,
Who rose as my phoenix out of the wild.

# Fear

Trying to heal can be a scary story.
Like digging in a granite quarry.
Your only tools are a teacup and spoon,
Hoping your life gets better soon.
Recalling things you've locked away,
In the hopes that soon it'll be a brighter day.
The child that hid all they were
Because dad didn't like that version of her.
Asking her mom after school,
We all knew the unsaid rule.
What kind of mood was dad in?
Should I hide it or can I grin?
Suddenly I jump 10 years.
Now I am facing teenage fears.
Not your typical sports and prom.
Isolation, survival, death and bombs.
Prepping for the end of the world,
Childhood dreams, shattered and hurled.
So far away, they've taken decades to find.
Lost and buried until she aligned.
Remembering before the pain,
To find yourself through the rain.
Relationships, they never worked.
This is where pain and violence lurked.
Decades have passed, you're healing it last.

It's time to put your fears to bed.
You know who you are, it's all in your head.
Don't be afraid. Take on your power.
Be the change now is the hour.
See the here and now, just observe,
Then take all that shit to the curb.
Throw out all fears and enjoy these years.
It's time to be bold, happy and sassy.
Have fun, live life, be confident and classy.
Squash the fears of rejection
Find your voice and make a projection,
To the world, and those you know.
You create that which you sow.
Speak your truth. Don't be shy.
All the lessons will apply.

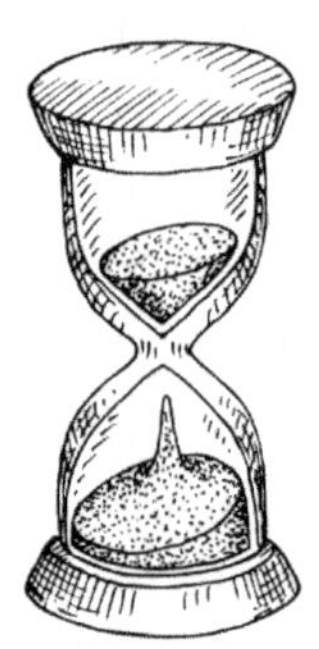

# Suicide

My brother, my friend, a man whose loyalty
knows no end.
Kind and generous is what he was, often times
just because.
There were no limits to the things he'd do, give
the shirt off his back if you wanted him to.
I've witnessed the pain and agony too, that of
which, very few knew.
Throughout his life, was confusion and strife.
And even as a child, this world was not mild.
Full of the harsh, cold, and unfair. For him, I
believe this is a breath of fresh air.
And though for those he's left behind, it's hard to
look at this as kind.
In my heart of hearts I know it's true, that in this
moment, his pain is through.
Although the void for us is raw, the agony of a
loss we never foresaw.
I take comfort in the knowledge that in God's
arms he'll find solace.
A peace and happiness he's never known, is all
we can ask that he will be shown.
A month before his day of birth, he saw fit to
leave this Earth.

# A Message From Mother Earth

Can you smell the smoke of the fires burning?
Or hear the sounds of your people yearning?
I hear their prayers, the same as before,
Begging for the sovereignty of promises you
swore.
The steady beat of their drumming,
And the sweet sound of humanity humming.
Broken by a sudden flash,
Of guns and cannons as they pass.
Have you learned nothing from events of the
past?
I fear not for you still hold the cast.
I breathed the breath of winter airs,
They stand there, freezing, with deep stairs.
The man-made snake is on its way,
To take my blood, for good they say.
You shave the trees from my land,
In order to shake another's hand.
Your heart, I see, is full of greed,
Clouding your judgment with its seed.
Consequences will soon be pending,
As you bleed my life, it's near the ending.
I once provided for all your needs,
But what have you shown me by your deeds?

Self-centered, righteousness and contempt.
Anger and violence are messages sent.
For bigger and better is all you care.
Financial gains, concerns you bear.
The value of the masses, no longer matters.
When profits decide, the community shatters.
You are left standing on an unstable landing,
When those you've left to struggle and die,
See through the fog of your grandest lie.
I cannot support the quantities you take.
Soon, my crust will begin to shake.
The empires you so decisively built,
Constructed on foundations, destined to tilt. I
send you the voices of the humble and weak.
They are coming together no longer so meek.
They see what you're doing,
And are no longer stewing.
Heard will be their voices.
You have one of two choices.
Listen to their cries,
Before humanity dies.
Or an end to this world, I will soon bring,
Destruction to all like you've never seen.

Yours Truly,

Mother Earth

www.ingramcontent.com/pod-product-compliance
Lightning Source LLC
LaVergne TN
LVHW050945200726
843508LV00011B/2444